W9-CBK-194

TYPES OF MUTUAL FUNDS

INFORMATION ABOUT FUNDS

INTRODUCTION

There are over 10,000 mutual funds managing over seven trillion dollars in investments for over two hundred million accounts. The phenomenal success of the mutual fund industry has made fund investing a serious element of most investment strategies. In Understanding Mutual Funds, you will learn what a mutual fund is, how it works, and why you would want to make mutual funds a part of your investment portfolio. It introduces you to ways in which you can analyze the goals and the risks of a fund, narrow your selection to a few without being overwhelmed by the many, and determine which fund or funds may be right for you.

GETTING STARTED

The first things you need to know about mutual funds are
what they are, why you might want to invest in them,
and how to choose the right one for you.

WHAT'S A MUTUAL FUND?

T he mutual fund is one of the
more ingenious inventions of
the financial industry. It allows small
investors to participate in virtually
any part of the financial world.

THE BASICS

A mutual fund collects money from a
lot of investors, and uses it to select,
purchase, and manage a *portfolio* (all the
investments owned by the fund) to
achieve a specific investment goal. A
mutual fund typically buys stocks,
bonds, and other types of securities. It's
a way for investors to be owners (stocks)
or lenders (bonds) by investing in many
securities at one time. Investors then
share in the capital appreciation and
income of those investments without
having to buy them directly.

GOAL: BUY A HOME

GOAL: PROTECT RETIREMENT SAVINGS

GOAL: TAKE A EUROPEAN VACATION

GOAL: PAY FOR GRANDCHILDREN'S COLLEGE TUITION

GOAL: BUY A NEW CAR

WHY BUY MUTUAL FUNDS?

Investing in mutual funds may offer you certain advantages over other types of investments.

Diversification. A mutual fund spreads your investment dollars around better than you could do by yourself. Spreading money among different investments is called *diversification*, which experts agree tends to lower the risk of losing money. The more types of investments a fund has, the more diverse it is. This usually results in less volatility, because gains from some investments in the fund offset losses from others.

Professional management. Many people don't have the time or expertise to make specific investment decisions. A mutual fund's investment managers are trained to make investment decisions to provide the best returns they can achieve based on the fund's stated strategy and goal. In essence, you get the services of a professional money manager without having to pay the high price of a personal manager.

Power in numbers. Putting your money together with other investors may help you achieve more than you could on your own by creating collective buying power. Together, you can buy a larger variety and quantities of certain investments.

Liquidity. This means you can easily sell your fund shares at any time and turn them back into cash.

THINGS TO KNOW

- You own part of the fund based on the amount you invest in it. If a fund has assets of $1 million and you invested $10,000, you own 1% of that fund. Each share you buy gives you a fraction of ownership in each investment the fund owns. Each share also has voting rights.

- Typically, the name of the fund will indicate what type of investment(s) the fund trades (buys and sells). For example, ABC Biotechnology Fund would most likely invest the greatest portion of its assets in biotechnology companies.

- The main disadvantage of owning a mutual fund is that as an investor, you don't have control over what the fund invests in. These decisions are solely the discretion of the fund's managers.

GOAL: GIVE MONEY TO CHARITY

DIFFERENT GOALS ▶ SAME GOAL

Many investors, each with different goals in life, can all channel their money into a mutual fund with the same investment goal.

THE RIGHT FIT

W*ith so many funds to choose from, how can you know which is right for you? First assess your own needs, then look only for funds that were designed to meet those needs.*

EVERY INVESTOR IS DIFFERENT

Every investor has different goals, desires, and kinds of risks s/he's willing to take. Virtually no two are alike. What helps you achieve your goals may not help others achieve theirs. The information here offers a start to your self-evaluation.

THE RIGHT FIT ▶
Your investment plan should be tailored specifically to fit you. The right fit for this investor, for example, means investing exclusively in securities issued in U.S. markets.

WHAT WILL YOU DO WITH YOUR MONEY?

In order to answer this question, you first need to ask yourself:

Where do I want to be? You have financial goals you want to achieve in your life. They may be things you want to buy, security in retirement, money for charity, or other things that are important to you.

How will I get there? You need to choose a strategy for achieving your goals. It should be based on whether you want to protect your money, grow it, earn income from it, or a combination of any or all of these goals. It should also be based on a specific timeframe. Different timeframes typically require you to use different strategies to achieve your goals.

What will get me there? Certain investments may be better suited than others, or have greater potential to help you achieve your goals.

What could stop me? Based on the strategy you choose, you will encounter different risks. You need to assess each risk to see whether it can be managed (meaning reduced) and whether it's worth taking (see pgs. 10-11).

IT's A FACT

Although there are more than 10,000 mutual funds in existence, they are managed by less than 400 investment management companies.

DECIDE WHAT TO BUY

Investors generally buy stocks for growth, bonds for income, and keep cash or buy money market securities for safety and liquidity. How you divide your money among these types of investments depends upon your answers to the four questions to the left.

Over the long-term, a diversified mix of investments can outperform a very conservative investment in money market securities or Treasury bills, and at the same time, avoids the higher risk of an all-stock portfolio.

A good investment plan should be based on four key questions that can be grouped under the bigger heading, "What will you do with your money?"

MANAGE YOUR PLAN AS YOU GO

Your plan doesn't have to be perfect from the beginning. Any investment plan usually needs to be adjusted over time. For instance, your goals, needs, wants, and risk levels will most likely change over time. They will be different when you're ready for retirement than they were when you graduated high school.

WHO OWNS WHAT?

- 63% of investors own at least two funds.
- 43% of investors own four or more funds.
- The average mutual fund investor has $18,000 in fund assets.
- The median age is 44 with a median household income of $60,000.
- 73% of fund investors own stock funds.
- 49% of fund investors own bond funds.
- 52% of fund investors own money market funds.
- 60% of fund investors purchased their funds through a broker, insurance agent, financial planner, or bank representative.

Source: Investment Company Institute Survey

YOUR RISKS OF INVESTING

Here are some risks every investor faces, regardless of the investment.

YOU COULD LOSE MONEY

This is, of course, the most obvious and feared risk of investing. There are, however, many strategies for managing this risk, particularly over the long-term.

YOUR MONEY MAY LOSE BUYING POWER

This risk is also known as inflation risk. It means that as prices increase, your investments need to increase in value at least at the same pace as inflation, so that you won't lose purchasing power.

For example, say you want to buy a car that's priced today at $20,000 but you want to buy it one year from now. So you put away $20,000 in a savings account which earns you 1% per year. If the price of the car inflates by 3%, you won't be able to afford the car next year. Your account will have $20,200 in it, but the car will now be priced at $20,600. It's as though you lost $400 by not purchasing the car this year. It's as though you actually lost $400 by earning 1% on your investment.

2 Setting an unrealistic goal may end up being your most detrimental risk.

YOU MAY NOT ACHIEVE YOUR GOALS

Probably the biggest, yet most overlooked risk of investing is the risk of not achieving your goal. It's probably overlooked so often because so few investors actually set goals, and many others unwittingly set unrealistic goals. Furthermore, many investors don't buy the right investments to help them achieve their goals.

This type of risk is often called *shortfall risk* (falling short of your goal). For example, if you have to invest for future college tuition, a money market fund might feel safe, but it's virtually guaranteed that you will fail and fall far short of reaching that goal.

MANAGING YOUR RISKS

Now that you know what risks you may personally take as an investor, be reassured that you can often manage these risks with some smart planning. Going back to the four questions on page 8, once you know what your goals and timeframe are, you can determine how much of each of these risks fits your investment plan. Some of these may be more important to you than the others. Be sure to consider them all.

3 The risks explained here are specific to you—the individual investor. They're different than the risks that are specific to mutual funds (see pgs. 30-31).

YOUR INVESTMENTS WILL RISE AND FALL IN VALUE

Almost all investments gain and lose value. This is known as *market risk*. In other words, the price of any investment, whether it's stocks, bonds, mutual funds, or any other, is likely to fluctuate (go up and down) over time. Seasoned investors tend to ignore daily movements in their investments, preferring to base their decisions on a longer-term view of their investments.

If you invest for longer periods of time, market risk may become less of a risk for you. That's because, over the long-term, prices tend to rise in most investments. Market risk, however, does become important to short-term investors who may need to sell at a time when prices happen to be down.

◀ **MANAGING RISK**
There are many different levels of risk and various ways of approaching those risks. For example, some people would never get on a pogo stick. Some people would get on it as long as they feel they're managing the risk by wearing a helmet and being sure their sneakers are tied. Some would take those precautions and have a lot of fun, while others would still be nervous but take the risk anyway.

A FUND FOR EVERY OBJECTIVE

There are over 10,000 mutual funds. Because many investors have different goals, risk tolerance, or strategies for achieving their goals, a wide array of funds has become available making it easy for most investors to choose one that will help them meet their needs.

EACH FUND HAS AN OBJECTIVE

Just as each investor has an objective, all mutual funds also have an objective (goal). This is the first way funds differentiate themselves from each other. They are generally divided into the following categories.

Aggressive growth. These funds are designed to aggressively grow assets. They invest mainly in stocks of companies with significant growth potential that haven't yet shown a pattern of growth. Their share prices can often be volatile. They're best suited for investors with relatively long timeframes.

Growth. These seek to grow the assets of the fund, but are less volatile than aggressive growth, and buy securities that have already shown a pattern of growth. They tend to be less risky than aggressive growth funds.

Growth and income. These funds tend to invest in both stocks and bonds. Stocks offer capital appreciation potential. Bonds are a safety cushion during volatile periods, while dividends and income provide extra capital appreciation. These funds are best for investors who need to balance capital appreciation with income.

Income. These funds tend to invest in bonds. They make money from bond income and any increases in the bonds' values. They fluctuate less in value than growth funds and are best for investors seeking lower risk levels.

Capital preservation. These funds invest in short-term investments, have the lowest risk of any of these categories and as such, offer the lowest returns. They pay investors from interest earned on their investments.

MANAGEMENT STYLE IS THE DIFFERENCE

Though objectives and strategies begin to differentiate funds from one another, the most important difference is each fund's management style. Style refers to the buy, sell, and hold decisions each fund manager makes based on criteria s/he believes are best able to help the fund achieve its objective. For example, one fund manager may identify the universe of stocks a fund may buy using a computer model, while the manager of a fund with an identical objective and strategy may compare stock prices to company earnings to identify potential selections.

EACH FUND HAS A STRATEGY

The second level of differentiation is strategy. For example, two funds may have the same objective of earning income. One may buy bonds, however, as its core strategy, while the other may focus on buying utility stocks with high dividends. You might select one fund over the other based on whether you want a steady income with few surprises in the value of your investment (the bond strategy), or you want to add a little more potential for price increases along with your steady income (the utilities strategy).

▼ THE SPECTRUM

Just as colors run through a spectrum, mutual fund objectives span a spectrum from aggressive (aggressive growth) to conservative (capital preservation). Some funds, however, have a combination of objectives.

EACH FUND HAS A FOCUS

Since the universe of investments is quite large, most funds are created with a certain focus.

Narrow focus. A fund may specialize in a narrow range of stocks. For example, it may invest mainly in stocks of wireless communications companies with market capitalizations over $5 billion that are traded in U.S. stock markets.

Broad focus. Another fund with the same objective and strategy might seek broader opportunities. For example, it may focus on any communications company, of any size, in any stock market worldwide. Doing so may add risks not found in the other fund, such as exchange rate fluctuations.

4 Mutual funds are meant to be longer-term investments. They are not designed to be bought and sold frequently.

WHAT MAKES FUNDS DIFFERENT?

With so many different funds to choose from, how can you sift through all of them to find the one that will help you meet your specific goal? Here's one way.

WHY CREATE FUNDS?

In general, a new mutual fund is created because someone believes it will fill an unmet consumer need, or that it has some characteristic that makes it stand out from the crowd. In short, every fund has been created in the hopes that it will become the choice for investors like you.

How you can pick funds. You can eliminate choices easily if you follow a method like the one this woman is using— a process of elimination from the most general qualities to the most specific ones.*

Goal. Her personal goal requires raising as much money as she can within 15 years.

Strategy. She has decided to allocate 15% of her money to a growth strategy, meaning that for that portion of her money, she wants to identify only funds that invest for growth. Most growth funds invest mainly in stocks.

What type? She's most interested in either high-tech companies or the most well-established companies (large cap stocks). She picks technology.

Where? Some funds invest only or mainly in U.S. companies; others in foreign stocks or a mix. She likes the foreign companies, and so, eliminates all the rest.

What region? She can choose emerging markets or European markets. She chooses emerging markets, believing they have greater growth potential. (Notice that she could have focused earlier on other funds investing in domestic companies regardless of industry and then selected a specific market capitalization. The order of preference depends largely on your own views.)

What management style? How does the fund manager make buy and sell decisions? What's the system? This is the level where differences become more personal.

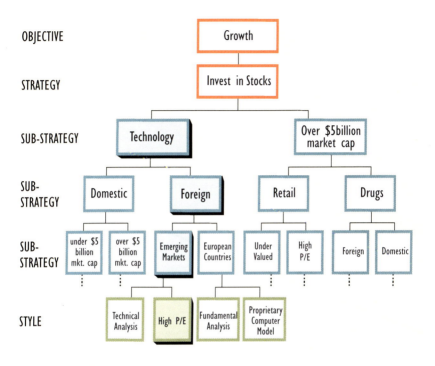

Style. There could be many more levels of management style that differentiate one fund from others. Style reflects the specific techniques a manager believes will work best to achieve the fund's objective.

5 There are enough funds to choose from so that investors can fine-tune their goals to meet their needs.

* This is only a simplified example. There are many variations on this scenario and it's only meant to illustrate a general analytical process.

HOW A FUND IS STARTED

Though anyone can start a mutual fund, very few have the ability to start one. It requires a tremendous capital investment and credibility to actually develop a fund to the point where it can be sold to the public.

HOW IS A FUND SET UP?

There are a number of different steps someone must go through to set up a mutual fund. Here's how.

1. The people who want to start a fund decide there is a market for a particular type of fund. Next, the fund must establish a distribution plan. They need to decide whether it will sell directly to the public and/or through brokers or other financial institutions. They put together a preliminary prospectus outlining the objective of the fund, strategies for achieving the objective, the management style, and other pertinent information.

2. The fund must then identify its custodian (the company that actually holds the fund's assets), who will do the accounting for the fund (meaning pricing fund shares and basic accounting functions), who the transfer agent will be, which attorneys will be representing the fund, and various other procedures that the Securities and Exchange Commission (SEC) must review before approving the fund shares for sale. Then it must submit everything to the SEC for registration.

3. According to the Investment Company Act of 1940, every fund must file a registration statement with the SEC. The SEC has very specific requirements for setting up a fund.

IT'S A FACT

As of the year 2000, nearly half of all U.S. households owned some type of mutual fund.

4. The proposed fund must then identify a board of directors, which must include *disinterested parties*. This means that none of these individuals can have any financial relationship with the fund or its affiliates (custodian, transfer agent, investment manager, etc.) The board of directors acts as a trustee for the fund's shareholders. They make all decisions regarding the operation of the fund, often with the assistance of shareholders through voting.

5. The directors then approve all the contracts, agreements, and resolutions for all the management personnel. A majority of disinterested directors must approve certain contracts in an effort to protect shareholder interests.

6. The SEC reviews the entire submission and sends it back to the fund for any necessary changes.

7. The fund makes these changes and returns the submission for final approval. It also puts the initial investment money into the fund so the fund has assets when it goes effective.

8. If there are no other changes, the SEC approves the registration, allowing the fund to begin operations.

6 Mutual funds must be registered by a state's securities regulators before they can be sold in that state.

NEW FUND ISSUES

There are a few issues a new fund needs to address which could present obstacles to getting started.

- How much will distribution cost?
- Where will it get the seed money?
- Does it have the credibility to hire management?
- Does it have a track record in investments?
- Can it pass the regulatory process?

OPEN OR CLOSED?

Open-end funds sell and redeem shares directly to and from investors at any time, Most funds are open-end funds. These funds are sold to investors at their current offering price. **Closed-end funds** issue a limited number of shares and are traded just like a stock on the stock markets. These shares may be offered at a discount or at a premium to the NAV.

HOW A MUTUAL FUND WORKS

Now that you know what a mutual fund is and why there are so many, it's important to know how they work and how to invest in them.

BUYING AND SELLING SHARES

There are a few different ways to buy and sell shares of a fund. Each fund has specific guidelines for how these procedures work.

WAYS TO BUY

Through a broker. Many funds sell their shares through brokers. Check with your broker to see if s/he can buy the fund you want. If you're able to buy through your broker, s/he will usually handle all the details of the purchase. If you buy through a broker you will pay a *load* (see pgs. 38-39).

Directly from the fund. Funds that sell their shares directly to investors typically advertise in financial magazines, financial sections of newspapers, in other financially related publications, or on TV. They usually offer an 800 number, which you can call to order a prospectus and receive other information. When you buy directly from a fund, you complete all the paperwork with the fund directly. If you buy directly from the fund you will pay the net asset value (NAV) (see pgs. 20-21).

From a bank. Many banks offer mutual funds, but their selection may be limited.

Through other sources. You may be able to buy mutual fund shares from financial planners, insurance agents, or other professionals who are licensed to sell securities.

FILL OUT AN APPLICATION

An application comes with a fund's prospectus. You may open an account with a mutual fund directly by completing the application and sending it back to the fund. The application asks for basic information including your name, the type of account you want to open, your Social Security number or tax identification number, and service option choices. Remember to send a check along with your application to the fund company.

EXCHANGING SHARES

Some funds allow you to exchange your shares for shares of another fund. This is usually allowed when you own shares of a fund that's part of a family of funds (see pg. 63). Most funds that allow exchanges, however, set limits on the number of times you can exchange shares without incurring any charges. Be aware that although there may not be a fee to exchange shares, there may be tax consequences associated with the exchange. Check your fund's prospectus for details about exchanging shares or call the fund's customer service number.

7 Keep the prospectus you receive from a fund for reference in case you have any questions later.

WAYS TO SELL

When you want to sell your shares, simply call the fund's 800 number or your broker and give them your instructions. Depending upon the fund's policies, and the options you chose when you completed your application, you may receive your money by check or wire, or you may leave the money in your account.

HELPFUL HINT

When you open an account, you're asked to choose various options for distributing money when you sell shares. Check as many options as the fund allows. This way, when you sell shares, you can choose whichever options are best for you at that time. Don't box yourself in by choosing options that won't allow you to access your money when you need it.

WHAT'S A SHARE WORTH?

T he value of a fund's shares may change every day because the values of the assets it owns may change daily.

WHAT'S THE VALUE?

The value of a share of stock changes based on supply and demand for that stock. It may have no easily recognizable relationship to the value of the company's assets. On the other hand, the value of a mutual fund share is specifically calculated based on the fund's assets, as shown here:

IT'S A FACT

According to the Investment Company Institute (ICI), fund pricing is almost 99.5% accurate. Lipper Analytical Services estimates the number to be closer to 98.95%

TOTAL
ASSETS

− EXPENSES

÷ NUMBER OF
OUTSTANDING
SHARES

———

NET ASSET
VALUE (NAV)

THE FUND CALCULATES THE VALUE

Net asset value (NAV) is the value of one share of a mutual fund. It's calculated Monday through Friday when the stock markets are open, at the end of each business day (usually 4:00 pm Eastern time). The fund adds up its total assets, subtracts expenses, and then divides by the number of outstanding shares in the fund.

THE FUND VALUES THE ASSETS

Each fund must adjust the price of its shares to reflect the current market value of the investments it owns. *Marking-to-market* is the industry term used to describe this process. All funds are required, by law, to perform this function each business day. Most use stock quotes to value their stock holdings, and will usually use market quotes for other types of investments where available.

THE VALUE (NAV) CHANGES

The price of a share is reduced when the fund pays out any distributions. This lowers the price of the shares, but you don't actually lose money because you receive the distribution either as cash or as a reinvestment according to your instructions on the application (see pg. 23). If you have cash sent to you, your account will have less money in it. If you reinvest the distribution into more shares of the fund, you will own more shares at a lower price and the value of your account will stay the same.

OOPS!

A mutual fund must submit its NAV to the National Association of Securities Dealers (NASD) each day. It is the NASD's job to distribute this information to news services. Every once in a while someone makes a mistake and gives the wrong number. Although this is rare, it says a lot about technology that wrong prices are usually detected and corrected long before any new shares are sold.

8 A fund purchases as many of its shares as your investment dollar amount allows. You may even own fractions of shares in a fund.

WHERE CAN YOU FIND A SHARE PRICE?

You can find the price of your fund's shares (its NAV) by looking in the financial section of your newspaper, calling the fund's 800 number, or searching for it on the Internet at the fund's website or other financial services sites. Ask your broker or the fund for the ticker symbol or abbreviation used in the newspapers or on the Internet. A fund's full name is typically too long to include in the listings. Many web providers now offer you the ability to track your investments by listing the ticker symbols of funds you own on your personal home page.

WAYS TO INVEST

There are at least three methods of investing your money in a mutual fund.

A LUMP SUM

You can make a one-time investment into the fund you select. Many funds have minimums. Be sure to check out the requirements of the fund you select. A fund may have no minimum for opening up an account, but still require a minimum investment to actually purchase shares of a fund.

AUTOMATICALLY

Most fund companies have investment plans which allow you to have money transferred automatically from your bank account or money market fund into one of their funds. You can find this option on the application form. **Voluntary accumulation plans.** These plans allow investors to buy small quantities of mutual fund shares on a regular basis. You open an account with a minimum investment of cash or mutual fund shares and make additional deposits on a regular basis, usually monthly or quarterly. The money in the account is used to buy the mutual fund shares you have selected.

A commercial bank usually administers the plan. When you mail in a deposit, the bank deducts a processing fee and purchases as many shares as possible with the balance.

A SPECIFIC AMOUNT EACH MONTH

With this method, called dollar cost averaging, you invest the same amount each month no matter what the NAV. This method is most appropriate for people who want a structured, disciplined investment plan and don't want to worry about trying to time the market for the best prices. Instead, their plan is to accumulate investment capital by avoiding any of the emotional decisions that often lead to procrastination.

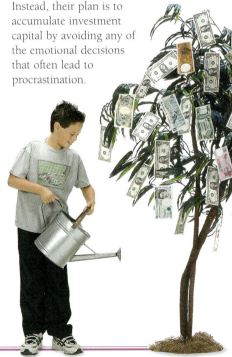

HOW YOUR MONEY GROWS

O*nce you've made an investment in a mutual fund, your money may grow in various ways.*

SHARE VALUES

As the value of the investments in the fund rise, so does the value of your fund shares. On the other hand, if the overall value of the investments goes down, so will the value of your fund shares.

CAPITAL GAINS

If the fund earns money when it trades shares, it will have capital gains. Funds are required to distribute these gains to shareholders. Most funds distribute capital gains once or twice a year. You may choose to have these gains automatically, reinvested in more shares of the fund.

COMPOUND GROWTH

If you choose to reinvest a fund's dividends, your money has *compounding* potential. For example, you invest $1,200 each year into a mutual fund (assuming an average return of 8% per year). After 20 years you would have about $46,000 versus about $28,000 if you chose to receive your dividends in cash. By reinvesting your dividends instead of spending them, you would have earned an additional $18,000. This is only a hypothetical example and assumes no taxes or expenses.

DIVIDENDS

If the fund receives dividends from bonds, stocks, or other investments it owns, it pays those out to shareholders as outlined in the prospectus. Dividends from a mutual fund may be either dividends earned from stocks owned by the fund or interest earned from bonds owned by the fund.

Fund distributions may be either short- or long-term capital gains.

Depending on your mutual fund, you may receive dividends monthly, quarterly, or annually. Capital gains distributions are typically made to investors once a year.

9 Any distributions an investor receives from a mutual fund are referred to either as dividends or capital gains distributions.

TAXES AND CONSEQUENCES

Selling or even owning shares of a mutual fund may have tax consequences. Here are some basic guidelines. As with any investment, check with your tax advisor about your situation.

WHAT'S TAXABLE?

You will only be taxed on money that's distributed to you by the fund. You will be taxed in the year the distribution is declared (whether you actually receive it or not that year). Here are the types of taxable distributions:

- Capital gains;
- Dividends.

You will also be taxed on any gains from the sale of your shares.

Keep in mind that:

- At least 95% of the money a fund earns must be distributed to investors in the year it's received;
- Each purchase and sale of fund shares is a separate transaction for tax purposes.

LONG-TERM VERSUS SHORT-TERM

The capital gains on your shares will either be taxed as long-term or short-term. Short-term capital gains are gains on shares you've owned for less than one year. Long-term capital gains are gains on shares you've owned for more than one year. The government rewards you for holding your shares longer by taxing long-term capital gains at a lower rate. Check with your tax advisor to know what your tax rate will be. It can be different for individuals at different income levels.

IMPORTANT DATES

There are important dates you need to be aware of for tax planning purposes when you own mutual fund shares. They are:

Declaration date. This is the date on which a distribution is declared;

Record date. Shareholders who own shares on this date will receive a dividend or distribution on the payment date;

Payment date. This is the date on which the dividend is actually paid;

Ex-dividend date. This is the date the shares trade without the dividend.

HOW TAXES WORK

To see how taxes work with a mutual fund, consider this example:

You own a fund whose NAV is $10.00. Of that amount, $1.00 per share is dividends that have been paid to the fund through its investments. It's December 31, 2001 and the fund has declared a distribution.

All investors. All investors receive the $1.00 distribution in their accounts.

Investors in tax-sheltered accounts. These investors may not have to pay any taxes at this time in accordance with the rules of their account.

Investors in non-tax-sheltered accounts. These investors are required to report the distribution on their 2001 tax return. Whether they receive the distribution in cash or reinvest it in more shares of the fund, the distribution is completely taxable. Even more important, whether or not investors receive the distribution in 2001 or 2002, it's still taxable in 2001. The important date here is the declaration date of the distribution.

10 Different tax rules apply when you hold fund shares in a tax-sheltered account such as an IRA or 401(k).

11 Save your statements from all of your mutual fund investments. You will need them for calculating your taxes.

HELPFUL HINT

When selling mutual fund shares, it's best to know the different methods of calculating what your shares are worth ahead of time. Some methods require that you designate which shares are to be sold before you actually sell them. For more information, call 800-TAX-FORM and ask for publications 544, 550, and 564, and schedules B and D. Remember, tax rules can change every year.

MORE ON TAXES

There are a number of tax scenarios unique to mutual funds. Knowing the potential pitfalls can help you avoid problems at tax time.

KNOW WHEN NOT TO BUY A FUND

It's very important to know when a fund is going to make a distribution. If you're buying and selling mutual fund shares in a tax-deferred or tax-free account, you don't have to worry about when you buy shares. Otherwise, here's what can happen.

A large distribution. Let's assume, for example, that on December 15 you invested $1,000 in a mutual fund. The fund has been doing quite well over the past five years and over the past six months has sold investments at a significant profit. Since the fund must distribute the gains from these sales by the end of the year, it makes a distribution, which for your shares is $100 or 10% of your total investment.

The consequences. You now have only $900 invested in that fund and also have a tax liability on the $100 distribution. You essentially bought yourself that tax liability. It doesn't matter whether you took the distribution in cash or reinvest it in shares of the fund. The only thing the IRS cares about is that you received the money and you owe taxes on it. You're essentially paying the government money on your own money! It may not seem fair, but that's the law.

12 Buying fund shares after it makes a distribution will lower the amount you pay per share. More of your money will be working for you.

KNOW WHEN TO SELL A FUND

Here are a couple of times it might be a good idea to sell a fund for tax reasons.

Starting over. If the manager of the fund you own decides to sell the fund's entire portfolio and start fresh, you may end up with a significant tax liability from capital gains. This could happen if the fund changes management.

Sell after the first of the year. If you wait to sell a fund until after the first of the year you won't have to pay taxes on any gains until the following year.

MARKETS CLOSED ▶
This investor has the right idea taking a taxable gain in the following year. The markets are closed, however, on major holidays.

AVOIDING UNWANTED TAX LIABILITIES

There are a number of things you can do to help minimize or eliminate your tax liability when you buy shares of mutual funds. You can:

- **Buy your shares through a tax-deferred or tax-free account.** This may not eliminate your tax liability altogether, but it's designed to help you pay taxes when you may be in at a lower tax bracket;

- **Examine the fund's holdings.** A fund may have certain investments it has held for a long time and may potentially sell soon, resulting in capital gains for you. Check the Financial Highlights table (see pgs. 46-47, "Net Distributions") to see if the fund has a history of large capital gains distributions. If so, you might

consider waiting until the fund sells those holdings so you won't be paying taxes on gains you didn't realize (see pg. 60 for how to view a fund's holdings).

- **Know when distributions will be made.** If you know a fund is making a distribution (as in our example on the opposite page), wait until after the distribution to buy shares. That way your money will buy more shares of the fund and you won't have to pay taxes on the distribution.

- **Consult with the fund manager.** Find out what the fund plans on doing with capital gains and dividend distributions, and when it plans on doing it. Giving this information to your tax advisor will help him or her help you make better investment decisions. After all, you're investing to make money, not pay money.

27

EVALUATING A MUTUAL FUND

The prospectus and other marketing materials make it easier to choose the right fund to help meet your goals. All the subjects covered in this chapter are in any mutual fund prospectus.

THE PROSPECTUS

To make it easier to evaluate and compare them, all funds must produce a prospectus.

YOUR GUIDEBOOK TO THE FUND

The prospectus is a document provided to you by the fund. It's a legal document required by the SEC to contain specific information. It covers all the relevant information about the company, such as its history, operations, financial conditions, and key personnel. It tells you the fund's objective, strategy for achieving the objective, potential risks, fees, costs, fund policies, how to buy and sell shares, and other information an investor would need to know before buying shares of the fund.

IT'S A FACT

During the late 1990s, the SEC revised the format for all prospectuses, making them more uniform. This makes it easier for investors to compare various funds. Now all prospectuses must be written in "Plain English."

13 Mutual funds are required by law to provide prospectuses.

IT MAY COVER ONE FUND OR MANY

A prospectus may cover one fund or a group of funds. If it covers many funds, each will have its objectives, strategy, risks, and other required information spelled out separately, unless all of the funds have exactly the same characteristics.

THE OVERVIEW

The opening section of the prospectus is called the *Summary*. It highlights the main objective of the fund, its primary risks, and the overall strategy for achieving the objective. It doesn't detail all of the relevant information about the fund. Instead, it lists the most important information that the SEC has deemed relevant for investors to make an informed decision about a potential investment in the fund. If you're still interested in the fund after reading the Summary, you should continue reading the rest of the prospectus to be absolutely sure you understand exactly what the fund is for and how it operates.

DATES

All the dates given in a prospectus relate to the date it was printed. In other words, if it says "the past 5 years," and the date listed on the front cover is April 29, 2000, it means that the 5 years referred to are 1995-1999. Check to see whether the fund uses a calender year or fiscal year for accounting purposes. This can affect your comparisons.

WHAT'S AN SAI?

A way to get more detailed information is to ask for a document called a *Statement of Additional Information* or SAI. This includes more details on accounting and other information than is found in the prospectus. Generally, the information given in the SAI is not likely to give you a better perspective on whether or not this fund is the right investment for you. Each fund is, however, required by the SEC to produce one and have it available to interested investors.

DIDN'T LEARN ENOUGH?

If, after you read the prospectus, you still want more information, ask your broker or a fund representative more questions. Especially when you pay a sales charge, you should take advantage of having a professional who understands the investment and can explain it to you.

RISKS SPECIFIC TO MUTUAL FUNDS

E very prospectus has a section covering the risks of investing in that fund. Marketing materials may not be as detailed regarding risks. Therefore, it's essential that you read and understand all the risks involved before giving any money to a fund. Each fund is different, so some or all of the following may be applicable to the funds you consider.

YOU COULD LOSE ALL YOUR MONEY

This is a risk all funds are required to tell you about. In most cases, this risk is very unlikely to occur. For a fund to go bankrupt, all the investments it owns must also go bankrupt. There's also the possibility that management could change and decide to liquidate the fund and distribute all the assets to you. In this case, you won't lose all your money.

VOLATILITY

Many things can cause the value of investments within a mutual fund's portfolio to go up and down. Changes in a company or industry, changes in the economy, or changes in investor's attitudes can all cause the value of investments to fluctuate. This type of risk is sometimes called *market risk*. If you're a long-term investor, this risk becomes less important, because historically, overall, investments have risen over time.

14 There are other risks of investing in mutual funds, but these are the main ones you can expect to come across.

FOREIGN INVESTING

You will see this risk discussed by any fund that buys investments from foreign countries. The main risks here are currency exchange rates, different accounting rules in other countries, and the possibility that something may happen in a country that would make your investment impossible to access, such as economic, political, or other changes (see pg. 60 for a more detailed discussion of the risks of investing in foreign funds).

DERIVATIVES

Some funds use options and other types of derivatives to manage risk within the portfolio. If the fund manager believes s/he can avoid losing money by buying derivatives to protect against a down market, then these "riskier" investments become a risk management tool.

INFLATION

A fund that focuses primarily on interest-earning investments will be negatively affected by inflation. As rates go up, the fixed amount of income these funds are earning has less buying power.

CONCENTRATION

When you invest in a fund that buys investments in one industry, your entire investment in that fund will likely suffer if that industry suffers a downturn.

CREDIT RISK

This the possibility a bond issuer may not be able to make scheduled interest and principal payments. If this happens, the overall dividend payments of the fund may be reduced. Independent rating agencies, such as Moody's and Standard and Poor's, rate larger bond issues to help investors identify and manage credit risk.

LIQUIDITY

If a fund buys securities of larger companies, it's more likely to be able to turn these investments into cash (liquidate) when and if needed than a fund that buys those of smaller companies. Stocks of companies with larger market capitalization are generally easier to liquidate. If a fund has difficulty liquidating its investments, its returns could be lowered.

INTEREST RATE

If interest rates change, that could adversely affect a fund's investments, particularly bond and money market funds, whose earnings are directly tied to interest rates.

COMPARED TO OTHER INVESTMENTS

No one can definitively say that investing in a mutual fund is less risky than investing in stocks or bonds. It all depends upon the type of fund you buy and your investment goals. It's generally believed, however, that a fund that buys many different types of investments lowers its risk level by diversifying its assets.

WHAT'S PERFORMANCE?

*A*fter you understand a fund's risks, you need to know how well it has *performed so far.*

WHAT THE FUND MUST TELL YOU

Each fund is required to tell you the percentage the value of its assets has increased in the past. Funds refer to this information as *performance* or *annual total return*. A fund is required to include up to 10 years of performance data (or the length of its existence) so you can compare it to other funds. The information must include:

- A bar chart;
- The actual performance number;
- The years covered;
- Any notes or other key information.

WHAT AFFECTS PERFORMANCE?

Just as anything can affect the price of a stock, virtually anything can affect a mutual fund's performance. The stock markets, the economy, social changes, or general investment attitudes can all cause a fund to perform well, or poorly. Generally, if there's a significant upturn or downturn in the markets, most mutual funds that invest in similar securities using similar investment strategies will have similar performance during a given year.

◀ KEEPING SCORE
How would you know who won the game if you didn't see the score? A fund's performance is essentially it's scorecard.

NO GUARANTEES

Every fund is required by law to tell you that past performance is no guarantee of future results. This means that just because the fund grew 20% last year, it does not mean that it will do that again this year. In fact, it may do considerably better or worse than that.

15 The front cover of any prospectus informs you that any fund that claiming it guarantees a specific return is committing a crime.

A WAY TO COMPARE

All funds are required to compare their performance to *benchmarks*. Benchmarks are indexes that are used by the industry and are considered to be good measures of how a particular segment of the market performed during a specific period of time. For example, a fund that primarily buys stocks of retailing companies may first use the Standard and Poor's 500 (a broad market index) to compare its performance to the market as a whole, and then to a consumer industry index to give investors a more comparable view of its performance compared to other funds that invest in the retail industry. (See pg. 36 for a more detailed discussion of using benchmarks.)

NOT GUARANTEED

Fund shares are not backed by or guaranteed by the FDIC or other government agencies. Funds may buy government backed securities, but that doesn't mean that the government is guaranteeing the shares of the fund. It's only guaranteeing the specific underlying shares that the fund has purchased.

HELPFUL HINTS

If you think a fund's performance is significantly higher or lower than the benchmarks and the reason is not readily apparent, be sure to read all the footnotes accompanying the performance information. If there's no reasonable explanation for the difference, the fund is either doing a better job of investing its assets, or the manager may not know what s/he is doing. Investigate thoroughly!

WHAT THEY DON'T HAVE TO TELL YOU

A fund that has been in existence for less than one year is only required to give year-to-date performance information. They can't give you what they don't have. If you're trying to compare a new fund with an old one, you will need to look at additional information. Consult an investment professional if you encounter this type of situation.

READING A PERFORMANCE CHART

T his is a sample of a performance chart you would find in a prospectus or marketing materials. Here's what it all means.

16 A load fund's reported performance is before sales charges.

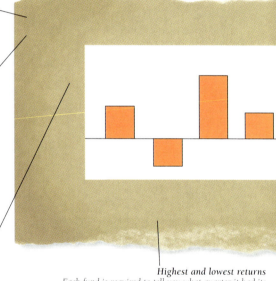

The name of the fund
Particularly if a prospectus is for more than one fund, the specific name of the fund will be given next to the bar chart.

The type of year
Most funds provide data by the calender year. However, some will provide data based on their fiscal year. Be sure you're using comparable data when comparing two funds. The difference between a calender and fiscal year can significantly affect the performance data a fund provides. Significant events may happen during a short period which may skew the information and make accurate comparisons difficult.

Percentages
The chart should give you a rising scale of percentages (most often on the left side). This is in addition to the actual percentage figure given at the top of the chart. It's all designed to make the information easier for investors to understand.

Highest and lowest returns
Each fund is required to tell you what quarter it had its highest and lowest returns. In other words, what were its best and worst quarters? It must also tell you the specific percentage increase or decrease the fund sustained during that quarter. You will typically find that these numbers correspond to significant events in the markets relating to the overall markets, or the specific industry represented by that fund. When you compare funds, check to see if the time periods for best and worst performance are the same.

WHERE ELSE CAN YOU FIND THIS INFORMATION?

The information on a performance chart may vary from fund to fund. If you don't find the information you're looking for, check the table of contents in the prospectus to see where that information is located. Even though funds are required to give comparable information, they may design and lay out their prospectuses and marketing materials quite differently.

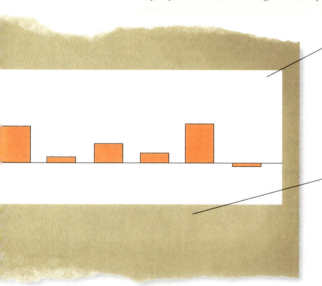

Actual percentages
Above (or sometimes below) a bar on the chart is the actual percentage of increase (decrease) in the fund's assets for the time period covered. In this example, during the calender year 1997, the fund's assets increased by 32.13%.

Year-to-date information
The fund must provide any year-to-date performance information. This is usually given as a footnote to the bar chart.

Footnotes
Any information which significantly affects the performance of the fund must be provided with the performance bar chart. Again, investors shouldn't have to search for information in order to make comparable comparisons between funds. Although this fund doesn't have any footnotes, you would typically find them below the chart.

WHAT THEY DON'T TELL YOU

Though it may appear that one fund performed better than another during a given period, the chart doesn't include any sales charges you may have incurred when you bought your shares of the fund. Remember that in order to make accurate comparisons, you must figure in how much you would have paid to buy shares of each fund.

AVERAGE ANNUAL RETURN

*A*ll funds provide information on how much your money has earned *over a given period of time. This information is different from fund performance and adds another way to compare various funds.*

WHAT IT IS

Average annual return is an average of a specific number of years (1, 5, and 10) of the fund's performance. *Total return* (given on the Performance Chart on pgs. 34-35) shows the actual annual increase or decrease in the fund's asset value for one year. Average annual return takes each year's total return and averages it over 1, 5, or 10 years and includes sales charges, which the total return figures do not.

WHY IT'S IMPORTANT

Every year's total return changes the average annual return. Therefore, one year of very high returns or one year of very low returns can make all the other years appear much better or worse than they really were. Look at the total return numbers on a fund's Performance Chart to get an accurate understanding of the actual year-to-year performance of a fund.

Mutual funds will advertise either their average annual returns or their latest total return for a specific period—whichever will look better for them. Pay attention!

17 Benchmarks give you a way to compare a fund to a part of the market or the whole market.

BENCHMARKS

Along with the average annual return data, you will find information explaining the benchmarks that are listed. The fund must tell you about each index so that you can decide whether it gives you enough of a comparison to make an informed investment decision. You can find indexes listed on many financial websites on the Internet or in many newspapers.

Name of the fund
Be sure you're looking at the correct fund if the prospectus you're reading contains more than one fund.

Years covered
The fund is only required to say "Past 1 year", "Past 5 years", or "Past 10 years" (or "Life of fund" if the data is for the life of the fund). Check the front cover of the prospectus to see what time period the data covers.

Footnotes
Read the footnotes at the end of the chart. They may provide information to help you make an accurate comparison of funds.

For the periods ended December 31, 1998	Past 1 year	Past 5 years	Past 10 years/ Life of fund
Utilities Growth	38.79%	20.18%	18.10%
S&P 500	28.58%	24.06%	19.21%
Goldman Sachs Cyclical Industries Index	4.74%	N/A	N/A

Broad market index
The first index listed is typically one that measures the overall market the fund invests its assets in, whether it's stocks or bonds. This gives investors an overall measure of how this particular fund has done compared to that market. If the fund's numbers are higher, the management is thought to be doing a good job of investing the fund's assets. If the fund's numbers are lower, the fund may want to reevaluate how it's managing its assets.

Industry index
These indexes are more specific measures of market performance. They track a similar segment of the market and are used to compare how well the fund did compared to the investments within that market segment.

N/A
This means that this index was not in existence during the period covered. This may be because the index is new. The fund may not provide a second benchmark if there isn't one that will provide a reasonably comparable measure.

18 Experts recommend investing in funds that have comparable or better than average annual returns to the market.

COSTS AND FEES

Though you aren't paying for a personal money manager, there may still be costs and fees for buying, owning, and selling shares. Be aware of these fees and compare them to fees of other funds before investing.

WHAT'S A COST?

Costs are what you pay for buying shares of a fund. There may be:

A sales charge. This is sometimes referred to as a *load* or *front-end load*. It typically varies from 1%-8.5% of your total purchase. It's used to pay commissions to brokers and financial advisors who sell the shares of the fund for the investment company. There's typically a sliding scale for loads: The more shares you buy, the less you pay;

No sales charge. Most funds that sell directly to the public are called *no-load*, which means they don't charge a sales charge;

A deferred sales charge. You might be charged when you sell your shares. Many funds have what is called a *Contingent Deferred Sales Charge* or CDSC. This is charged if you sell your shares within a specific time period. Many funds have a sliding scale for the CDSC so it completely disappears after a few years if you continue to hold the shares;

Other costs. Some funds charge maintenance fees for accounts below a minimum balance or other miscellaneous charges.

WHAT'S A FEE?

Fees are what you pay the fund manager for its expertise and the expenses of the fund. Fees are paid out of the fund's assets, not directly from your account.

Marketing expense fees. These are called *12b-1 fees* and are used to pay the marketing expenses of the fund. This can mean distribution, promotions, commissions to brokers who sell the fund, or advertising expenses. It may be as large as 1.25% per year of the total assets of the fund.

Management fees. These are the fees which pay for the managers' salaries and expertise for managing the fund.

Other fees. There may be other operating expenses for the fund, such as administrative costs, which are passed on to investors.

THINGS TO KNOW

If you know how long you plan on holding shares, you may be able to save yourself some money.

● If you plan to hold shares for a short time (less than 7 years), no up-front fee but a greater annual fee makes more sense.

● If you plan to hold shares for a long time (more than 7 years), paying more up-front and less annually makes more sense.

LOAD FUNDS

Why buy a load fund? Buying a load fund is like shopping at a full-service broker. You pay a premium, but in return you get investment advice. The premium (or load) you pay is used to compensate the broker for that advice, just like a commission on a stock purchase. It all depends upon your needs.

Load versus no-load. There are no significant differences between the performance of load and no-load funds in their operation or success.

A load can cost you. A load of $475 on a $10,000 investment means that only $9,525 of your money goes to work for you (instead of your full $10,000 in a no-load fund). If the fund appreciates 12%, your account would be worth $342,420 after 30 years. If you invested $10,000 in a no-load fund, the account would be worth $359,496. In effect, that $475 sales charge cost you $17,076.

PORTFOLIO TURNOVER

What is it? This is a measure of how actively a fund manages its investments and how much it buys and sells those investments.

What does it mean? A ratio of 150% means a fund with $100 million of assets sold $150 million worth of investments in 12 months.

What is normal? Turnover ratios may run 10% in some index funds to over 500% for some bond funds and aggressive growth funds.

What is a good rate? A high or low turnover ratio isn't good or bad in itself. Some funds' styles call for frequent selling, while others call for very low activity.

What is the downside? Because buying and selling securities costs money through commissions and spreads, a high turnover indicates higher costs (and lower shareholder returns) for the fund. Also, funds that have high turnover ratios will end up distributing yearly capital gains to their shareholders.

Which fund do you choose? If all else is equal when comparing funds, a low turnover ratio means lower expenses (commissions) for trading and lower taxes for shareholders. A fund that has a high portfolio turnover will have more capital gains distributions than a fund with low turnover, because the low turnover may mean that the fund has unrealized gains.

THE FEE TABLE

*E*ach fund has specific fees and must provide investors with a fee table that can easily be used to compare it with other funds. The fees will vary with each fund. Although the amounts and percentages may be different, here's a typical fee table.

Maximum sales charge
This is the most you can be charged to buy shares of the fund. The footnote tells you that if you have an account with more than a $250,000 balance, you may receive a reduced sales charge.

Sales charge on reinvested distributions
If you reinvest your distributions, you will not incur a charge with this fund.

Deferred sales charge on redemptions
You will not incur a sales charge when you sell shares of the fund.

Redemption fees
You will be charged when you sell your shares. The longer you hold the shares, the lower the fee. You may pay as little as $7.50.

Fee table
Shareholder Fees (paid by investor directly)

Maximum sales charge (load) on purchases (as a % of offering price)[A]	3.00%
Sales charge (load) on reinvested distributions	None
Deferred sales charge (load) on redemptions	None
Redemption fee for the stock funds (as a % of amount redeemed)	
on shares held 29 days or less	0.75%
on shares held 30 days or more	0.75%
for redemption amounts of up to $1,000	0.75%
for redemption amounts of $1,000 or more	$7.50
Exchange fee	
for the stock funds only	$7.50
Annual account maintenance	$12.00

[A] *Lower sales charges available for accounts over $250,000*

Exchange fee
You may be charged an exchange fee for exchanging shares of one fund into another.

Annual account maintenance fee
If you don't maintain the minimum balance the fund requires, this fund will charge you $12.00 per year.

ARE 12B-1 FEES GOOD OR BAD?

Some people say 12b-1 fees don't benefit existing investors because they simply reduce fund performance. Others argue that by advertising and bringing in other investors, and thus more assets, the fund's buying power increases and can improve its performance. Check these fees carefully to see whether what is being charged is worth the benefit to you.

ANNUAL OPERATING EXPENSES

F*unds are required to list all expenses as a percentage of the total assets of the fund. These expenses are usually paid monthly. Here's a typical annual fund operating expense table.*

Distribution and service (12b-1) fee
This particular fund does not charge a 12b-1 fee.

Other expenses
This fund charges 0.75% of the total assets of the fund annually for other expenses.

Management fee
This fund manager charges 0.59% of the total assets of the fund each year as its fee for advising and managing the fund's portfolio. If you divide this amount by 12, you will get the amount that's paid out each month. The more important figure, though, for comparison purposes, is the annual percentage. Each fund must list these fees in this format.

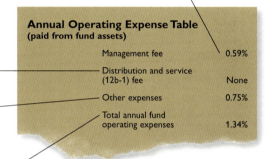

Annual Operating Expense Table (paid from fund assets)	
Management fee	0.59%
Distribution and service (12b-1) fee	None
Other expenses	0.75%
Total annual fund operating expenses	1.34%

Total annual fund operating expenses
Add up the top three figures to get this one.

THINGS TO KNOW

- Stock funds tend to be the most expensive with annual expenses from 0.2% to 3%. Most are between 1% and 1.5%. Small company and international funds tend to be more expensive, because they cost more to trade.

- Money market funds tend to be the least expensive. Their expenses typically run between 0.2% and 1.0%. These funds do not typically charge loads.

DIFFERENT SHARE CLASSES

Some funds have different classes of shares. Each share class owns the same thing, but they all have different costs and fees. For example, *A* shares typically have upfront loads, while *B* shares typically don't. However, the *B* shares may make up for the difference by charging higher fees. *C* shares typically charge deferred sales charges, or none at all if you hold the shares long enough. Be sure you understand which shares you're buying, and why, before you send any money.

THE FEE EXAMPLE

The SEC requires each fund tell you how much it will cost to own shares of a fund. The example assumes you invest $10,000 in that fund and earn a return of 5% per year. This is the best way to compare fees from fund to fund.

Account opened
This is the amount you would pay in expenses if you left your investment in the fund.

Account closed
This is the amount you would pay in expenses if you sold your shares of the fund.

The Year
The example tells you what you would pay out of your investment in expenses if you hold shares of the fund for 1, 3, 5, or 10 years. It doesn't matter how long a fund has been in existence. All funds must project these amounts based on their current expense figures.

The amount
These are actual dollar amounts, as opposed to the fee table which lists the percentages of total assets used to calculate expenses.

			Account Opened	Account Closed
Air Transportation	1 year		$433	$441
	3 years		$715	$722
	5 years		$1,017	$1,025
	10 years		$1,875	$1,883
Automotive	1 year		$443	$451
	3 years		$745	$752
	5 years		$1,068	$1,076
	10 years		$1,983	$1,991
BioTechnology	1 year		$432	$440
	3 years		$712	$719
	5 years		$1,012	$1,020
	10 years		$1,864	$1,872

19 Every fund must use the same format for the fee example. This makes comparing funds very easy.

REFUNDING FEES

A fund manager may reimburse a fund for its expenses if the expenses exceed a specified amount. This is one way funds keep their returns up and attract investors. A fund is required to state this in its prospectus.

INVESTMENT POLICIES

E *ach fund must provide more detail regarding its strategies and specific policies. You will find all this information in the prospectus, usually after the summary. As with much of the other information, the SEC requires all these details be disclosed to investors so they can compare funds and be fully informed before making any investment decisions.*

WHAT YOU STILL NEED TO KNOW

By now you know the fund's objective and strategy for achieving that objective. If the fund has not provided detailed information in its summary, it must still disclose in more detail:

- What types of investments the assets are primarily invested in;
- The percentages of how the assets are divided;
- Whether the fund can invest in foreign assets, derivatives, or other types of investments;
- What defensive techniques the fund may use to protect its portfolio from downturns in the markets;
- What type of analysis a fund manager may perform to make its buy and sell decisions;
- Whether a fund is diversified or non-diversified;
- Whether the fund may lend securities to others in order to earn money for the fund;
- Whether there are any legal proceedings pending against the fund;
- Any other information the SEC believes is relevant for investors to be able to make an informed decision.

20 Most people are inclined to skip the details section of the prospectus. It may, however, contain details that are not in line with your investment philosophy. Read it carefully.

WHAT'S DIVERSIFIED AND NON-DIVERSIFIED?

A *diversified fund* is one that invests no more than 5% in one company and 25% in one industry. A *non-diversified fund* may invest up to 10% in one company and 25% in one industry. Just because a fund states that it's non-diversified, in practice it may keep its investments diversified. The designation simply allows it the freedom to invest the assets in a non-diversified way.

MANAGEMENT OF THE FUND

P ossibly the most important factor in determining how well the fund may perform in the future, is who is managing its assets. You need to carefully evaluate whether these individuals have investment philosophies your like and the experience you believe will be able to achieve the objective of the fund.

WHAT MANAGERS DO

The fund manager is responsible for making all the investment decisions for the fund and supervises its day-to-day operations. This includes:

- Buying and selling investments;
- Monitoring the portfolio daily;
- Analyzing existing investments;
- Analyzing potential investments;
- Evaluating the fund's strategy and how it's working;
- Interacting with the fund's Board of Trustees on matters involving the operations of the fund;
- Any other functions which are deemed necessary for the fund to achieve its objective.

WHO MANAGES THE FUND?

The fund may be managed by:

- One or several individuals;
- An investment firm, who designates specific individuals to oversee operations;

It may also be *advised* by an individual or group other than its managers.

WHAT THEY HAVE TO TELL YOU

The SEC has specific requirements that each fund must disclose to you regarding the people in charge of its investments. They must tell you:

- The name, title, and length of service of each portfolio manager and that person's business experience over the past five years;
- What the advisor's specific role is in the management of the fund, and what that role is relative to the manager's function;
- The name and address of each advisor;
- The advisor's experience;
- What services that advisor provides for the fund;
- What each advisor gets paid and how that amount is calculated.

21 Check to see how long a fund manager has been in charge of the fund. Its performance is closely tied to the individual(s) who manage it.

22 Make sure the manager has a good back-up in case s/he decides to leave. A manager's departure could be detrimental to a fund's ongoing performance.

HOW THEY GET PAID

The base pay. Managers are paid a fee for their services. This is usually a percentage of the assets they manage. Some funds may pay their managers set fees or other specified compensation. **The incentive.** They may also have incentive clauses in their contracts that reward them if the fund performs at or above a certain level. Since a manager is paid a percentage of the assets s/he is responsible for, there's an automatic incentive to do well for investors. If the fund performs well, it will hopefully attract more investors, meaning more money to manage, and in turn—if it continues to do well—more fees for a job well done.

WHAT TRAINING DO THEY HAVE?

Fund managers tend to be people who have worked in the investment industry and have proven themselves to be knowledgeable in a particular area. They may have previously worked as:
- Stockbrokers;
- Analysts;
- Traders;
- Other investment managers.

If the manager has no previous investment experience, it's probably a good idea to check out his or her resume in the prospectus more carefully. You want to make sure someone with investment experience is managing the fund.

DON'T BLAME THE MANAGER

Growth and value stocks tend to move up and down in cycles, leading and lagging each other every couple of years. So you should be aware that a growth stock fund that is doing well will naturally go in and out of favor, regardless of its management.

FINANCIAL HIGHLIGHTS

A fund that has been in existence for more than one year is required to give investors a Financial Highlights table. Here's what all the information means.

Fiscal or calender year
It's important to know whether the Financial Highlights for a fund are given for a calender year or a fiscal year. A fiscal year is a time period covering one year that the fund uses for accounting purposes. If it uses a fiscal year which ends any time other than December 31, your comparisons with a fund that uses a calendar year (all calendar years end December 31st), may be inaccurate. This fund uses a fiscal year ending on February 28th. (February 29th on leap years).

Per-share data
All the information given in this table is per share, not for the collective fund. That means that each piece of data given directly relates to what happens to each share you own.

Net asset value, beginning of period
This is the NAV that the fund starts out its fiscal year with. That means that on March 1st, this is the NAV that was quoted to investors who wished to purchase shares that day.

Income from investment operations
This section details all activities of the fund that resulted in money being earned from the fund. It includes any dividends, interest, or capital gains earned from investments in the funds portfolio. The total figure simply takes the income (loss) and adds (subtracts) gains (losses) to arrive at the total income the fund earned.

Less distributions
This accounts for any money that was distributed to shareholders during that particular year.

Net asset value, end of period
By adding up all the other data you get this number, which tells you what shares of the fund were valued at on February 28th of that year.

Financial Highlights

LEISURE

years ended February 28,

Selected Per-Share Data

Net asset value, beginning of period

Income from investment operations

　　Net investment income (loss)[C]

　　Net realized and unrealized gain (loss)

　　Total from investment operations

Less distributions

　　From net realized gain

Redemption fees added to paid in capital

Net asset value, end of period

Total Return[A,B]

Ratios and Supplemental Data

Net assets, end of period (000 omitted)

Ratio of expenses to average net assets

Ratio of expenses to average net assets after expense reductions

Ratio of net investment income (loss) to average net assets

Portfolio turnover rate

[A] *The total returns would have been lower had certain expenses not been reduced during the periods shown*

[B] *Total returns do not include the one time sales charge*

Total Return
This tells you what percent shares of the fund increased during that year. This is after all expenses have been paid.

Ratios and Supplemental Data

Analysts use many measures to evaluate the financial information provided by a fund. Funds are required to give you certain ratios so you can see that, for example, the expenses have been in line with what the fund advertises. By giving you ratios, you can become your own analyst and compare this fund's financial data with another fund's.

1999	1998	1997
$62.30	$47.83	$46.17
(.27)	(.25)	(.06)
22.78	21.10	4.47
22.51	20.85	4.41
(3.44)	(6.46)	(2.83)
.07	.08	.08
$81.44	$62.30	447.83
37.54%	47.29%	10.14%
$346,139	$257,199	$98,133
1.26%	1.44%	1.56%
1,24%	1,39%	1,54%
(.40)%	(.46)%	(.12)%
107%	209%	127%

[C] *Net investment income (loss) per share has been calculated based on average shares outstanding during the period.*

Net assets, end of period
In this table, (as with most) the fund has listed the total net assets of the fund (not a per share amount), and has left out three zeroes (000). This is strictly for convenience. They do this so they can fit the numbers into the table.

Ratio of expenses to average net assets
Use this ratio to determine if the fund is keeping its expenses in line with what it advertises them to be. Hopefully, over time, you will see this figure going down. In this case the fund is realizing economies of scale by reducing its expenses as assets increase.

Ratio of expenses to average net assets after expense reductions
Some funds have reimbursement agreements with various third parties (see pg. 42 for a more detailed discussion of expense reimbursement). You can see in this example, that although the reimbursement only slightly reduces the expenses, it does have an effect on the bottom line.

Ratio of net investment income (loss) to average net assets
This tells you what percent of the average net assets was gained (lost) through the activities of the fund.

Portfolio turnover rate
See page 39 for a full discussion of portfolio turnover rates. Unless the fund is a money market fund, it is required to give you a portfolio turnover rate.

Footnotes
Pay particularly close attention to any footnotes accompanying the Financial Highlights table. They may hold the key to unusual returns, ratios, or other important figures you are basing your investment decisions on.

TYPES OF MUTUAL FUNDS

There are many different types of funds designed to meet different objectives. This chapter describes the most common categories you will see. Remember, though, that funds may be combinations of a few types of funds.

MONEY MARKET FUNDS

These funds are considered among the safest places to invest your money.

WHAT IS IT?

Money market funds loan money on a short-term basis—from overnight to one year. They earn interest on the money they lend. They primarily lend money to government entities.

Money market funds make low risk loans and earn low interest. They are, therefore, considered low risk investments. These funds are different from other funds in that they try to maintain a constant NAV of $1.00. They do it by paying out all income to shareholders.

WHY BUY THIS FUND?

Investors typically put money in a money market mutual fund when they want to protect their money. They earn income from a fund's investments, but money market mutual funds tend to have the lowest returns of any mutual funds. The only investments they generally outperform are traditional bank savings accounts.

Use Overnight

WHAT'S A REPURCHASE AGREEMENT?

It's a contract in which the seller of debt securities, usually Treasury Bills, agrees to buy them back at a specified time and price. It's also called a buyback, and is used to raise cash and enhance the return on other investments.

23 Park your money in a money market fund while deciding where you want to invest.

MAIN RISKS

The main risks of investing in money market mutual fund are:
- Credit risk;
- Interest rate risk.

Fresh for One Month

DIFFERENT TYPES

Money market mutual funds come in many forms.

Regular funds invest in short-term debt of all types;

Government funds invest only in national government or government agency debt or repurchase agreements involving such debt. This carries a slightly lower credit risk than regular funds.

Treasury funds invest only in direct obligations of the national government or repurchase agreements involving these securities. They carry the lowest credit risk and dividend distributions are exempt from state income taxes in most states.

Municipal funds invest only in debt of state or local governments. For most individuals, dividend distributions are exempt from national income taxes.

Single state municipal funds invest only in debt of one state or its political subdivisions. For people who live in that state, dividend distributions are exempt from federal income taxes and that state's income taxes. A single state fund is usually less diversified than a regular municipal fund and might be considered riskier for this reason.

NO GUARANTEES

Unlike money market bank accounts, an investment in a money market mutual fund is neither insured nor guaranteed by the FDIC or any other government agency. Unlike bank CDs, the yield isn't fixed. In other words, when interest rates rise, the fund's yield should also rise, and when rates fall, the yield should also fall.

STOCK FUNDS

S tock funds tend to be the most common types of mutual funds. While they primarily invest in stocks, most also buy other types of securities.

WHAT IS IT?

A stock fund is one that mainly invests in stocks. It may buy common or preferred stocks. It may focus on one or many segments of the stock market, depending upon the objective and strategy of the fund.

MAIN RISKS

Depending upon the type of stocks a fund buys, any or all of the risks discussed on pgs. 30-31 may apply. Read the prospectus of your specific fund to understand its risks. The stock a fund buys may have different risks than the fund that buys it.

WHY BUY A STOCK FUND?

You would buy a stock fund if you're looking to grow your initial investment. It's important to match a particular stock fund with your investment objectives and risk considerations.

HOW IT WORKS

The manager of a stock fund analyzes stocks that meet the criteria of that particular fund. Referring back to the model on pg. 15, a fund may have several layers of criteria for choosing stocks. Here's an example:

Broad strategy. If a fund invests primarily in large cap companies, the manager will look for stocks s/he believes will outperform other large cap stocks.

Narrow strategy. The fund can narrow its focus by investing primarily in large cap U.S. computer companies, and narrow it further by focusing only on stocks that are undervalued based on technically analyzed charts. The manager will look for stocks s/he believes are poised to outperform the rest of the industry based on these factors.

Stock funds often hold small amounts of money market investments or cash to meet redemptions. Some hold larger amounts of money market investments when they can't find enough stock worth investing in or if they believe the market is about to head downward.

DIFFERENT TYPES

Stock funds invest based on different criteria.

Capitalization. A stock fund may invest based on market capitalization. It may invest in micro-, small, mid-, or large cap companies.

Industry. It may invest in one industry or sector.

Country. It may invest in one or many countries, or a specific region of the world.

Analysis. It may make investment selections based on fundamental or technical analysis. It may also use specific *systems* or computer models.

Objective. A stock fund may be aggressive growth, growth, income, or growth and income. You won't find a stock fund that has protection as its objective.

Within each one of the categories listed above, a fund may combine smaller segments of that category to achieve its objectives. For example, a fund may invest in micro-cap stocks, or it may buy micro- and small cap stocks. Some categories overlap naturally, but some funds invest across categories because they can better achieve the fund's objective. For instance, a fund that buys micro cap stocks may be buying software stocks, while a software fund may buy micro cap, or restrict itself to small cap stocks.

24 The subcategories of funds represent how funds have developed to achieve their objectives more effectively.

25 Different types of funds may have different methods for defending against down markets.

WHAT'S A SECTOR FUND?

A sector fund is one that invests primarily in a group of industries that have similar interests. For example, a high-tech sector fund may invest in biotechnology, wireless communications, software, semiconductors, and personal computers. It can allow you to diversify among a variety of industries to take advantage of a growing segment of the economy.

BOND FUNDS

Many people avoid bond funds because they believe they're difficult to understand. With a professional managing the fund, you mainly need to understand the objective, risks, and investment philosophy of the fund.

WHAT IS IT?

A bond fund is one that primarily invests in bonds. Bonds are loans to corporations or governments (usually called debt). Whoever buys a bond is lending money in exchange for receiving regular interest payments until they're repaid their original investment.

MAIN RISKS

The main risks of investing in bond funds are:
- Interest rate risk;
- Credit risk;
- Volatility.

> **26** Bonds may be *called*, meaning the borrower can pay off the loan ahead of schedule, which removes a source of income from the fund.

WHY BUY A BOND FUND?

You buy a bond fund if want to earn income. The fund you choose depends upon a balance between the amount you want to earn and the risk you're willing to take. Bond funds provide a more predictable source of income than stock funds and can also grow in value.

HOW IT WORKS

Here are some important factors to consider:
- **Yield.** This is the percentage of your investment (paid out as dividends) that you earn as interest;
- **NAV.** If interest rates drop, the NAV of the fund will tend to rise. If rates rise the NAV will tend to fall;
- **Average maturity**. This is the average number of years until the bonds end (mature). Generally the longer the average maturity, the higher the yield;
- **Credit rating.** Generally, better credit ratings of the fund's bonds means lower yields but higher stability.

While you may buy a fund for its yield, be sure to look at its NAV. It can change the same as any other mutual fund's NAV, as the value of the bonds in the fund change in value. There's the risk, therefore, that your investment may be worth less when you need to sell it, and could even erase gains you may have earned from interest.

LADDERING

Laddering is an investment method used by bond fund managers. A manager buys a set dollar amount of bonds with set maturities at specified intervals (such as once a year). Buying bonds this way reduces risk by lowering the volatility of the yield. It doesn't, however, allow for any defensive measures by the manager in a down bond market.

DIFFERENT TYPES

Bonds can be grouped at least two ways. One is by maturity. Generally, the longer the maturity, the higher the interest rate risk because there's more time for rates to fluctuate.

Short-term. This type of fund usually buys bonds with less than 5 year maturities. It typically has a low interest rate risk.

Intermediate-term. This type of fund usually buys bonds with 5-15 year maturities.

Long-term. This fund buys from 15-30 year average maturity bonds.

Bonds can also be grouped by the type of issuer. Generally, credit risk is a concern.

Corporate. When you invest in a corporate bond fund, you're lending your money to a corporation.

Government. In these funds, you're lending money to a government entity.

Municipal. With municipals, you're lending money to state and local governments and their agencies.

You may also hear about mortgage-backed securities and adjustable rate funds. These funds buys bonds that support home mortgages. If you intend to invest in these types of funds, consult an investment professional because they can be complicated.

GRADING BONDS

Bonds are rated primarily by Moody's and Standard and Poor's rating services. Bonds rated A+ through B are usually considered *investment grade* and have a lower credit risk associated with them. Fund managers are generally restricted to investing within certain bond ratings as part of the stated strategy of their fund.

BALANCED FUNDS

Some funds combine different types of investments to achieve their objectives from a different angle.

WHAT IS IT?

This fund mixes stocks and bonds. A typical balanced fund might contain about 50-65% stocks and the rest in bonds. It's important to know the ratio of stocks to bonds in a fund to understand the risks and rewards inherent in that fund.

MAIN RISKS

Depending upon the type of investments a fund buys, any or all of the risks discussed on pgs. 30-31 may apply. Check with the fund manager to see which risks specifically apply to the fund you're interested in.

WHY BUY A BALANCED FUND?

You buy a balanced fund when you're looking for growth and income but want to be protected during down market periods. The bonds provide income, while the stocks provide capital appreciation potential. The bond portion of the fund adds stability, protecting investors when stocks are out of favor or during volatile periods.

HOW IT WORKS

By mixing stocks and bonds (and sometimes other types of assets) a balanced fund is likely to give a return between that of stocks and bonds. The risk of investing in this type of fund is usually less than investing in either a stock or bond fund alone. These funds will usually show lower returns than growth funds alone, during rising market periods, but will also most likely show less downside during a downturn in the market.

27 These funds attempt to minimize risk without sacrificing the possibility for capital appreciation.

28 Be aware of a particular fund's definition of balance. Some funds may allow the scales to be tipped more in the direction of stocks than bonds creating a higher level of risk.

DIFFERENT TYPES

Balanced funds are essentially asset allocation models. As such, they may be divided into two categories. They may be either:

Regular balanced funds. These funds usually keep their ratio of stocks to bonds fairly constant.

Asset allocation funds. These funds may switch the ratio of stocks to bonds. The changes are usually based on market timing: when it appears better to own bonds or stocks.

WHAT THEY USUALLY BUY

Balanced funds tend to buy relatively high grade bonds and tend to diversify more in stocks than other funds. By doing so, they lessen the risk of the overall fund. The manager is still able to make defensive purchases to protect the fund, but must stay within specific boundaries as stated in the prospectus. Read the prospectus carefully to determine how strict the parameters are.

RISK CONSIDERATIONS

Some funds may try to improve their performance by:

Pushing stock ratios to the limit. Some funds may be allowed to invest up to 75% of their assets in stocks, leaving only 25% in bonds. This is not considered a well-balanced fund;

Buying lower grade bonds. Some funds may buy low grade bonds because they pay a higher return. This, however, exposes the fund to a higher level of risk;

Buying higher risk stocks. Some funds may invest a significant portion of their assets in aggressive growth stocks. This also creates an unbalanced fund.

It's important to know what the fund you buy can do to improve its performance. You can find this information in the details section of the prospectus, where the fund lists its investment criteria. A fund's investment policies may not be in line with your tolerance for risk. Investigate thoroughly.

TAX-RELATED FUNDS

Many funds are set up to shelter assets from taxes or simply buy investments that are free from taxes. Check with your tax advisor to see if one of these funds will benefit you more than a taxable fund.

WHAT ARE THEY?

Mutual funds may offer taxable or tax-free income. The term *tax-related funds* is used here to mean any funds that have specific tax issues associated with them. They may be called tax-free, tax-exempt, tax-sheltered, or tax-advantaged.

MAIN RISKS

Depending upon the type of investments a fund buys, any or all of the risks discussed on pg.s 30-31 may apply. Check the fund prospectus to see which risks specifically apply to the fund you're interested in.

> **29** Your year-end statement will show in detail how much of your gains are taxable.

> **30** A taxable fund may be easier on your taxes than a tax-free fund. Check with your tax advisor.

WHY BUY TAX-RELATED FUNDS?

You buy a tax-related fund when you're looking to protect your income from taxes or when you want to avoid paying taxes altogether on your investment earnings.

HOW THEY WORK

Recent changes in tax laws have narrowed the options for the average investor to shelter investment earnings from taxes. If your objective is tax-free income, there are mutual funds that invest in municipal bonds or tax-exempt notes. There are some mutual funds that produce income that's exempt from income taxes in certain states. Tax-exempt funds are typically identified as *municipal bond* funds or *tax-free* funds.

DIFFERENT TYPES

Municipal bond funds. These funds buy bonds issued by state and local governments and affiliated entities. Income earned by these funds and paid to residents of the issuing bond's state are free from federal, state, and any local taxes. That's why you may sometimes hear a bond referred to as "triple tax-free." If, however, you invest in a municipal bond fund that buys bonds issued by a state other than your home state, the income you earn will be taxable.

Tax-free funds. These may be municipal or state funds. You won't be charged taxes on any earnings if you live in the state in which the bonds owned by the fund have been issued.

Government bond funds. These funds invest mainly in bonds issued buy the federal government. A portion of the income earned may be taxable, depending on the situation. The interest earned may be exempt from state taxes but not from federal taxes.

MUTUAL FUND OWNERSHIP OF MUNICIPAL SECURITIES

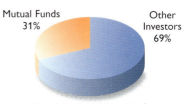

Mutual Funds 31%

Other Investors 69%

Total Municipal Securities Outstanding: $1.53 trillion

▲ WHO OWNS BONDS?
At the end of 1999, according to ICI and the Federal Reserve Board, mutual funds owned 31% of the municipal bonds in the market. Other investors owned the remaining 69%.

31 While a fund may be exempt from federal income taxes, it still may be subject to state and local taxes.

BUYING MUTUAL FUNDS IN AN IRA

Most funds have what is called a *custodial arrangement* for IRA shareholders. If you buy shares for your IRA directly from the fund using a custodian (a company that takes care of all the administrative tasks of buying the shares for your IRA), you must use a special application available from the fund company. The custodian usually charges $10 to $15 per fund account per year. You can purchase mutual funds through the broker that holds your IRA. You usually are charged a custodial fee of between $25 and $50 per year. Custodial fees are usually paid separately from your yearly contribution, and may be tax deductible. Call 800-TAX-FORM for general IRS information about IRAs. Remember, tax laws are constantly changing, so be sure your information is up to date.

INDEX FUNDS

There are funds specifically designed to follow indexes such as the Dow Jones Industrial Average or the Nasdaq Composite Index. These funds aren't managed the way other funds are, and thus have different fees.

WHAT IS IT?

An index fund tries to equal the returns of a particular segment of the market by buying the same securities as a specific index tracks. This type of fund is often referred to as a *passive* fund (as opposed to an *active* fund) because decisions are made in response to market movements and no fund manager is needed to make buy or sell decisions. The stated objective of most index funds is to approximate the returns of the index it's following.

MAIN RISKS

An index fund can't use defensive mechanisms to guard against losses in a down market because the fund is designed to do whatever the market does. As with any other fund, the securities the index fund buys also have risks that are specific to those investments.

WHY BUY INDEX FUNDS?

You would buy an index fund if you were looking to pay lower fees for a mutual fund and wanted to buy a fund that followed a particular segment of the market as measured by a specific index. An index fund is usually considered fairly diverse (lowering risk), because it may buy hundreds or even thousands of stocks.

WHAT'S AN INDEX?

Indexes are actually numerical calculations, based on groups of investments. The resulting numbers are meant to give investors the overall price level of a given market. For example, there are indexes for blue chip stocks, small stocks, foreign stocks, Treasury Bonds, etc. Some examples are the Dow Jones Industrial Average, the Standard and Poor's 500 index, and the Russell 2000 index.

32 Index funds have lower fees than other mutual funds because they aren't actively managed.

TRACKING THE BENCHMARK ▶
This is a typical chart illustrating the performance of an index fund compared to the performance of the index it was designed to mirror. In this case, the LTX Index Fund is comprised of the same large cap stocks that are part of the S&P 500 index, which is the most widely watched indicator of large cap stock performance.

How They Work

An index fund buys all the securities covered by a given index based on the weighting given to each security within that index. It attempts to match the market so that the returns of the fund will match (as closely as possible) the increase or decrease in the index it's designed to mimic. These funds don't in any way try to do better than the index they track.

Because of transactional costs and redemptions in the fund, all index funds must hold a portion of their assets in cash.

An Exact Match?

Though an index fund is set up to equal the index it follows, there's one catch. No index fund is capable of exactly matching its index. The actual index is a computer model that assumes you could always turn each security into cash at any moment (also known as *perfect liquidity*), and it doesn't take into account any fees.

Different Types

Each index fund is different, because each one owns different segments of the market. For example, a Dow Jones Industrial Average fund owns the 30 stocks in that index, while an S&P 500 index fund owns 500 different stocks.

The Controversy

Some investment professionals argue that investing in an index fund is a better investment than an actively managed fund: You avoid high fees and the potential for bad management you might encounter in other mutual funds. Others argue that an actively managed fund can protect against downturns in the markets that an index fund cannot. It's very important that you thoroughly investigate all the gain and loss potential of either type of fund in order to make sound investment decisions no matter what your views.

Average Annual Total Returns as of 12/31/00

	1 Year	3 Year	5 Year	10 Year	Since Inception	Inception Date
LTX Index Fund	13.38%	16.44%	21.63%	19.29%	15.19%	08/31/86
S&P 500 Index	13.28%	16.44%	21.69%	19.44%	---	---

FOREIGN FUNDS

There are funds for investors who want to own securities trading in foreign markets.

WHAT IS IT?

A foreign fund is one that mainly buys securities issued in foreign countries. It may be a stock or bond fund or a combination of both.

WHY BUY FOREIGN FUNDS?

You would buy a foreign fund if you were looking to invest in growing commerce in other areas of the world. For example, you may know about a type of technology or trend that seems to be emerging from somewhere else and want to take advantage of it. You also may want to manage your risk by investing in a fund rather than one specific company.

HOW THEY WORK

A foreign fund works the same way as any other fund. It may, however, buy the direct securities of a company, or it may buy ADRs (see box), which reduce risk.

DIFFERENT TYPES

A foreign fund may invest in:
● A specific region or country;
● Emerging markets, such as Singapore or Thailand;
● Aggressive growth stocks;
● Developing countries (those that are growing in economic power).

MAIN RISKS

The risks associated with foreign investments are quite different than any other types of funds. The main risks are:
● Accounting differences;
● Currency exchange rates;
● Political differences;
● Economic differences.

WHAT ARE ADRs?

American Depository Receipts (ADRs) are certificates which represent shares of a foreign company. They make it easier to buy securities of foreign companies, because they're traded on U.S. exchanges using U.S. dollars. Without ADRs, an investor must buy foreign shares through a foreign stock market in that country's currency, after exchanging U.S. dollars for that currency.

UNIT INVESTMENT TRUSTS (UITs)

*S*ome funds buy securities and hold on to them instead of trading in and out of them the way other mutual funds do.

WHAT IS IT?

A Unit Investment Trust (UIT) is a type of fund that buys specific securities and holds them for a set amount of time. This time period is called the life of the trust. A UIT doesn't trade any of the securities during the life of the trust. It holds onto them for better or for worse.

MAIN RISKS

The main risks of investing in UITs are:
● Liquidity;
● The lack of protection against price declines in the investments the trust owns.

WHY BUY A UIT?

You would buy a UIT if you believed the specific set of securities it owns, will help meet your investment objectives. A UIT also offers stable income. Since it doesn't trade its investments, the income remains as stable as the income of the investments it owns. As with other mutual funds, a UIT may give you the ability to buy specific stocks and other securities you might not otherwise be able to buy enough of on your own.

HOW IT WORKS

A fund company announces it has set up a UIT and advertises to potential shareholders which securities it will buy. UITs are generally closed-end funds (see pg. 17). Once the trust has enough investors (usually on a specified date) it closes and then purchases the investments. It then holds onto them for the specified time period. At the end of the life of the trust, investors are given the choice to redeem shares or reinvest them into additional shares of a new UIT. Most trusts will renew and set a new maturity date for the new trust. At that point, after evaluating the performance of the trust to date, the manager may decide to sell some securities and buy others.

OTHER TYPES OF FUNDS

T*hese are funds designed to meet the specific interests of some investors.*

SOCIALLY RESPONSIBLE FUNDS

These funds restrict their investments to whatever they define as socially responsible. They may avoid investments in:

- Military products;
- Alcohol;
- Tobacco;
- Animal tested products;
- Gambling industries.

Different funds have different investment and social criteria, although they usually prefer investments in companies that treat their employees and the environment well.

DON'T GET CONFUSED

You may hear that a fund is *closed*. Be aware that *closed* is not the same thing as a *closed-end* fund. A fund that is closed is one in which the manager has decided it can't manage the fund's assets as effectively if it takes on more investors. It feels that the investment objectives of the fund are better served using only existing funds and not taking in any more investment dollars. These funds may, however, sometimes sell more shares to existing shareholders.

OPTION FUNDS

These are high-risk investments in which the manager of the fund buys and sells securities known collectively as *derivatives*. Although these types of investments may be used to try to limit upward or downward movement, buying a fund that invests strictly in these securities should only be done by investors who completely understand the risks involved. In fact, in order to buy one of these funds, most brokers or funds ask you to sign a form stating that you understand the risks of investing in these types of securities. Though the potential for return is great, so are the risks.

DUAL PURPOSE FUNDS

A dual purpose mutual fund is a closed-end fund that invests equal dollar amounts in income producing securities and capital appreciation potential securities. You either buy the income shares or the capital shares.

Income shareholders receive a set, minimum rate of return and are paid all of the dividend and interest income (less expenses) produced by the fund. Income shares are redeemable at a stated time and price. Income shareholders don't receive any part of the fund's capital growth.

Capital shareholders, on the other hand, receive no periodic income, but are entitled to all the fund's assets after the fund terminates and the income shareholders have been reimbursed.

REAL ESTATE INVESTMENT TRUSTS (REITS)

These funds were developed for people who want to invest in real estate, but aren't willing to take on the risks involved in limited partnerships. REITs offer a more liquid and flexible way to invest in this market. Real estate is known for increasing in value over long periods of time. Though it may experience temporary downturns, long-term investments in real estate are looked at favorably by experts. These trade just like stocks on the stock exchanges.

NATURAL RESOURCES FUNDS

These funds are becoming more popular. They invest primarily in energy, oil, wood, and gas products. The reason for these funds is a belief that natural resources are a good asset allocation. We will always use energy and products that "come out of the ground," so these funds want to take advantage of an ongoing need.

WHAT'S A FAMILY OF FUNDS?

A family of funds simply refers to a mutual fund company that offers many different types of funds. This has certain advantages for both investors and the company. Families of funds sometimes offer:

● Additional services, such as easy switching from one fund to another (sometimes by phone) within the family. With load fund families, switching from one load fund to another is sometimes allowed without paying a second load;

● Some families may make bookkeeping easier by listing all of an investor's different funds on one statement;

● Others reduce expenses by sharing services, which helps them realize economies of scale.

Note, however, that the advertised performance of one fund in a family may or may not be shared by others.

INFORMATION ABOUT FUNDS

There are many places to find information on mutual funds. This chapter will help you track down these resources and use them wisely.

RESEARCHING A FUND

There are many ways to research information on a mutual fund. Here are the most common.

WHERE TO FIND INFORMATION

For information on no-load funds, you have many choices. You can look in newspapers, financial magazines, on the Internet, or in other publications from specific services that offer financial information. Brokers and financial advisors offer fund information, but they usually cover only load funds—the one's they sell.

MUTUAL FUND REVIEWS

Many periodicals have regular mutual fund review issues. Some of the best are:

- Barron's (quarterly);
- Money Magazine (Nov.);
- Business Week (Feb.);
- Forbes (Sept.);
- Fortune (fall);
- Consumer Reports;
- The Wall Street Journal;
- Investors Business Daily;
- Morningstar Mutual Fund Report;
- Value Line Mutual Fund Survey.

MAILINGS FROM THE FUND

Prospectus. This is a guide to understanding your fund (see pg. 28). Though you should have already read it before investing, the fund will send you another one after you invest. It's required to do so by law.

Statements. You will receive statements from your broker or the fund not less than quarterly, and you may receive them monthly. The statement details all transactions, including any purchases, sales, dividends, and any other distributions. It shows what your account is worth and what funds are held in your account. If you buy a fund through your broker, the broker's clearinghouse will receive the statements and add the information to your account so that you get your information on the fund along with all your other brokerage account records.

Year-end summary. You will receive a year-end summary and should keep it as long as your account is open. For tax purposes, you should keep statements for three years.

THE INTERNET

Websites. There are many websites where an investor can find virtually all of the information necessary to make an informed choice about mutual funds. For example, try:

● Quicken.com;
● Smartmoney.com;
● Fundstyle.com.

Chatrooms. Many web services and mutual fund websites offer chat rooms where investors can compare notes with other investors on mutual funds.

Online research. Aside from the companies that offer the funds, there are many websites which offer analysts views on funds. Try typing the name of a fund into any search engine. You're likely to get a list of the research on that fund, as well as the fund's own website.

ATTENTION 401(K) ACCOUNT HOLDERS

401(k) investors don't receive prospectuses for each fund. The plan sponsor (the employer) receives the prospectuses and the information is then put into something called a *Summary Plan Description* (SPD), that's distributed to all participants.

DIFFERENT INFORMATION

Different periodicals and books use different criteria to rate funds. These periodicals and books usually have phone numbers which you can call to get a fund's prospectus and other information. Note that some ratings account for loads, while others don't.

IT'S A FACT

Investments in mutual funds went from $1 trillion in 1990 to more than $7 trillion in 2000.

ANNUAL AND QUARTERLY REPORTS

E ach fund is required by law to send each of its investors annual and semi-annual reports, and quarterly statements. These are great sources of information on the past performance of the fund and have other valuable, comparative information.

ASSET ALLOCATION- ▶ LIST OF HOLDINGS

This is a document you will receive from the fund each quarter. It lists in detail the securities that the fund held on the last day of the period covered by the report.

CHANGES IN ▶ NET ASSETS

This is a more detailed version of the top portion of the Financial Highlights table. It tells you what the assets of the fund were worth at the beginning of the period, what occurred that changed the value of the assets, and finally, what the assets were worth at the end of the period. The Financial Highlights table in the prospectus only gives you annual information, while this gives you more detailed quarterly information.

	Shares	Value (000s)
RETAIL 6.0%		
Retail 2.5%		
Autozone, Inc.	350,00	11,309
Circuit City Stores, Inc. Circuit City Group	499,500	22,509
Office Depot, Inc.	900,000	9,844
PETsMART, Inc.	6,080,000	34,960
Systemax Inc.	887,700	7,545
Growth Capital Partners I, L.L.P.	52,500	165
		86,332
		209,106

	Amounts in thousands	
	1999	1998
Increase (Decrease) in Net Assets		
Operations		
Net investment loss		
Net investment gain	$(40,228)	$(35,087)
Change in net unrealized appreciation	449,948	614,899
Net increase in net assets resulting from operations	231,028	(574,200)
	640,748	5,612
Distributions to shareholders		
From net income	—	—
From net realized gain	$(512,373)	$(499,865)
Total distributions	$(512,373)	$(499,865)

	Amounts in thousands (except per share amount)
ASSETS	
Investments in securities at value (including repurchase agreements of $510) (cost $1,888,741)	$3,459,437
Cash and cash equivalents	350
Receivable for investments sold	41,227
Receivable for fund shares sold	926

◀ **INCOME STATEMENT**
This tells you what the fund earned, what it spent, and in the end, what it was able to distribute to shareholders (the net realized gain).

	Amounts in thousands
Total Income	**25,939**
Expenses	
Investment advisory fee	50,897
Distribution fee	12,215
Shareholder servicing fees	3,937
Service fees	1,025
Dividends on securities sold short	561
Audit fees	459
Custodian fees and expenses	438
Interest expense	437
Printing and mailing expenses	294
Non-interested director's fees and expenses	239
Legal fees	160
Registration fees	50
Miscellaneous expenses	623
Total expenses before reimbursement	71,335
Expense reimbursement by investment advisor	
Net Expenses	**66,167**
Net Investment Loss	**$(40,228)**
Realized and unrealized gain Net realized gain on:	
Investment securities	$448,454

◀ **BALANCE SHEET**
This is a list of the mutual fund's assets (what the total value of the investments in the fund are worth), liabilities (what it owes), and shareholders equity (assets minus liabilities—how much the shares of the fund collectively are worth).

IT'S A FACT

The Investment Company Act of 1940 requires all funds to register with the SEC, while the Securities Act of 1933 mandates specific disclosures by funds to its shareholders.

33 Reviewing the "Asset Allocation - List of Holdings" will tell you whether a fund invests in companies you like.

34 These reports give you more insight into the workings of a fund and whether it meets your investment criteria.

EDUCATION AND PROTECTION

The SEC has set up specific guidelines for the operations of mutual funds. If you suspect any problems, you can turn to one of these organizations for help and guidance.

WHO TO TURN TO FOR HELP

Contact any one of these organizations, if you have questions that the fund, your broker, or anyone else you're dealing with regarding mutual funds can't answer, or if you feel you've been wronged during a transaction.

Securities and Exchange Commission (SEC). Just as it regulates all other securities activities, the SEC monitors and regulates all mutual fund activities. You can find them on the Internet at www.sec.gov.

National Association of Securities Dealers (NASD). The NASD regulates sellers of securities. Any mutual fund company, broker, or other entity that sells shares of mutual funds comes under their jurisdiction. You can find them on the Internet at www.nasd.gov.

State securities regulators. Each state has its own organization for regulating the securities that are sold in its jurisdiction. Check with your local government office for ways to contact the regulators in your state.

 35 Use rating service information to supplement the prospectus information.

IT'S A FACT

The Investment Company Act of 1940 requires fidelity bonding of officers and employees of a mutual fund company, annual audits by outside firms, that detailed semi-annual reports must be filed with the SEC, and that shareholders must receive periodic financial reports.

ACCOUNT PROTECTION

The Securities Investor Protection Corporation (SIPC) protects investors' accounts from a fund or broker going bankrupt for up to $500,000 per account. Though the likelihood of either of these entities going bankrupt is quite small, it's good to know that you're insured in case of an extreme situation. SIPC doesn't insure you against losses in the value of your account due to normal investment activities. More importantly, as with any investment, there are no guarantees of success.

RATING SERVICES

To help investors learn more, a number of ratings services have been created to compare mutual funds. Lipper and Morningstar are the most widely used by investment professionals. They provide information on:

- The manager's name and tenure;
- Major individual investment holdings;
- Overall portfolio characteristics (such as the amount of stock in various industries, bond credit ratings, etc.);
- Performance information that's easily compared on an "apples-to-apples" basis with other funds and with indexes. For example, a fund's performance will be compared on a chart with other, similar funds, and with comparable indexes of similar investments (i.e., in general, a foreign fund's performance will be compared to the overall performance of foreign stocks).

Morningstar is an investment research and information company based in Chicago, Illinois. They have a mutual fund information service called Morningstar Mutual Funds, which has become a standard for mutual fund research.

Lipper Analytical Services is a service similar to Morningstar, and has been in the industry for many more years.

No-Load Fund Analyst is just like its name implies—it analyzes no-load funds.

INVESTOR EDUCATION

The Investment Company Institute (ICI) is the national association for the mutual fund industry. It seeks to enhance public understanding of mutual funds, to encourage the highest ethical standards by all segments of the industry, and to promote the interests of fund shareholders. As of 2000, its membership included 8,239 mutual funds, 489 closed-end funds, and 8 sponsors of unit investment trusts. ICI represents its members and their shareholders regarding legislation, regulation, taxation, public information, economic and policy research, business operations, and statistics.

36 Because of the protection of the SEC, SIPC, and other regulations, it would be difficult for an officer or employee of a mutual fund company to commit a crime that would affect your investment in that mutual fund.

37 Mutual fund shares are held by a custodian to protect investors from potential fraud.

69

INDEX

ACKNOWLEDGMENTS

AUTHORS' ACKNOWLEDGMENTS

The production of this book has called on the skills of many people. Marc would like to thank George Henning of Pacific Global Advisors for his expert input concerning the content and his generous willingness to do whatever was asked of him. This book is considerably better for having his involvement. We would also like to thank our editors at Dorling Kindersley, and our consultant, Nick Clemente. Marc wishes to dedicate this book to Zachary Robinson for his great patience and support when it was most needed.Special thanks to Teresa Clavasquin for her generous support and assistance.

PUBLISHER'S ACKNOWLEDGMENTS

Dorling Kindersley would like to thank everyone who worked on the Essential Finance series, and the following for their help and participation:

Writing Stephanie Rubenstein; **Design and Layout** Jill Dupont;
Consultants Nick Clemente; Skeeter; **Indexer** Rachel Rice; **Proofreader** Stephanie Rubenstein;
Photography Anthony Nex; **Photographers' Assistants** Damon Dulas;
Models Tom Dupont, Harold Rose, Zachary Robinson, Joshua Tohl, Jane Cho;
Picture Researcher Mark Dennis; Sam Ruston

AUTHOR'S BIOGRAPHY

Marc Robinson is co-founder of Internet-based moneytours.com, a personal finance resource for corporations, universities, credit unions, and other institutions interested in helping their constituents make intelligent decisions about their financial lives. He wrote the original *The Wall Street Journal Guide to Understanding Money and Markets*, created *The Wall Street Journal Guide to Understanding Personal Finance*, co-published a personal finance series with Time Life Books, and wrote a children's book about onomateopia in different languages. In his two decades in the financial services industry, Marc has provided marketing consulting to many top Wall Street firms. He is admitted to practice law in New York State.